Lessons I Learnt From My Mother

Lessons I Learnt From My Mother

Bamidele I. Kehinde

iUniverse, Inc.
Bloomington

LESSONS I LEARNT FROM MY MOTHER

iUniverse books may be ordered through booksellers or by contacting:

iUniverse
1663 Liberty Drive
Bloomington, IN 47403
www.iuniverse.com
1-800-Authors (1-800-288-4677)

ISBN: 978-1-4620-5043-7 (sc)
ISBN: 978-1-4620-5044-4 (ebk)

Printed in the United States of America

iUniverse rev. date: 09/07/2011

This book is dedicated to the loving memory of my dear mother, Olusola Oladele Kehinde. And also to my Dad—Julius Kolawole and my siblings—Oluwadamilola, Ayodeji and Ifedayo.

1

On the 6th of March 2011 when my mama died, I thought my world had come to an end. "How can God allow this", I thought to myself. I had never been so close to experiencing such an incidence in my entire life. I have always heard of people dying but this was the first time I would be right beside a dying person. She died in her sleep.

This day goes down in the history of my life because it was the least expected that happened to me. For three good years, we battled for my mother's life after the doctors diagnosed breast cancer. It was very traumatic for us to see her emaciate, lose all the hair on her head, take different tablets of drugs like she was drinking water, and have swollen legs that she couldn't even lift anymore. Oh! It is even very difficult for me to write all these things as they are making memories to flood back. I am still trying to do my best to get over her death despite the fact that it is over two months now.

However, I know somehow within me that she will be happy I am writing this book because she had always been a full supporter of my writing skills. She never discouraged me in all my endeavours. Maybe because she was just playing her role as a good mother should or somehow, she knew her time was so short that she had to make the best use of it.

This book is dedicated to her because she was very instrumental in making me who I am today. I wish I had written this while she was alive but all the same, I am happy that my siblings, Dad and

I never failed as much as we could to give her compliments and praises as at when due when she was alive. We all knew that our mum was one of a kind, a woman who had so many good virtues that even we her children, are still trying so much to emulate.

During the burial ceremony, people turned up as if we were honouring a celebrity. This really touched my heart. I felt like the daughter of a virtuous celebrity. Not many celebrities these days are virtuous. So many people gave gifts. Likewise, they poured in so much encomium. I was stunned by the different groups of people who came around to register their condolences. I saw a lot of elderly people cry which I had not seen in years. I thought, "Oh, so elderly people/grownups too do cry, I felt it was only children and teenagers that did".

However, it must be mentioned that there were a lot of pieces of advice from different people. Some even made it look as if death was an everyday thing to them—how inconsiderate they were in their manner of advice. Family members stood by us but they all dispersed sooner than we expected. This just made my siblings and I to know that we need to brace up for the challenges ahead. A shocking discovery in the process of hearing these various pieces of advice was the realization that three particular women (who were my mother's friends) had lost their mothers at very tender ages. This was shocking because I never knew all this while that they had to grow up without their mothers. I could not believe that I am now experiencing what they had to go through at much younger ages than mine. I then told myself that if these ones could make it with divine help, my siblings and I could make it even better than they did.

It is not easy to lose one's mother especially at a tender age in one's life. The role of a mother can neither be quantified nor overemphasized. Across all the countries in the world, everyone knows that the mother usually has immense impact and influence on the family (children) than the father does. This is not to slight the fathers/men but just to state the obvious. Writing a book about the lessons learnt from my mother does not mean I never learnt anything from my father, it is just that the mother's roles are more prominent and easily come to fore in my everyday living. Out of the three particular women mentioned earlier, it is only of them who really overcame the devastating effect that a mother's death bestows on someone. The other two overcame the shock but lived lives that are void of a mother's positive influence on a child. It was in the process of analyzing these women's lives that I came to the conclusion that the lessons my mother taught me must be well guarded in my heart and made use of appropriately. I told myself that all her efforts, teachings, moral lessons, etiquette lectures, marital advice must never be thrown to the winds.They are more precious to me than having all the gold in the world. Gold has price but pieces of her great advice are very priceless and inestimable.

As result of this, I decided to put into writing as many of these lessons that a book can contain as they are too numerous to be handed down in one book. Moreso, as mentioned earlier, writing these lessons of life will not only be a constant reminder for me but will invariably be sort of a guide for as many women there are across the world who will lay their hands on this book. Infact, this book is meant for both genders—male and female because we all need to keep learning lessons about life for as long as we live. Learning is a continuous process for the human minds.

In addition, I want this book to be made use of by mothers who consciously or unconsciously have neglected handling down the right lessons of life to their children, it is never too late. Train up a child in the way of the Lord and when he grows, he will not depart from it and of course, you will have peace of mind. In the next chapter is the biography of my mum as paraphrased by me. It is important to do this so that you holding this book will know that you do not need to be so extraordinary before you can be of great influence on your children. It just takes the ordinary woman to do extraordinary things. After all, we have history being replete with stories of mothers who were ordinary citizens but through their influence and impact produced extraordinary children. An example who readily comes to mind is the mother of the famous John Wesley. Other examples include the mother of Ben Carson, the grandmother of the great American president, Barrack Obama, Mother Theresa who had so many nonbiological children, the mother of the Nigerian Afrobeat maestro—Fela Anikulapokuti and a host of others.

A Nigerian adage says that a child is what you put into him. That is, teach your children well so that you will see them turn out to be the type of children you desire to have.

2

My mum Olusola Oladele Kehinde was born on the 20th of July, 1957 to the family of Late Pa Samuel Kolawole Fapohunda and Madam Olamieye Fapohunda. She was the first child of the family with other siblings. Due to the migratory nature of her father's job, she had her primary education in three different schools and attended two secondary schools before she could have her secondary school leaving certificate.

As a result of her love for education as a profession, she proceeded from obtaining higher school leaving certificate as it was then to teacher's training college. She also completed her Nigerian Certificate in Education (NCE) course before the quest to move higher academically prompted her to go further in her studies. In 1992, my mum gained admission into the highly esteemed University of Ibadan in the southwestern part of Nigeria to study Linguistics/Yoruba in the Department of Guidance and Counseling. She finally bagged her Bachelor of Education degree in the year 1998.

Even as she was getting all these qualifications, she had to make sure the home front was okay. My mum got married to my Dad—Julius Kolawole Kehinde on the 28th of August, 1982. Funnily, I usually celebrate my birthday before their annual wedding anniversary as I was born on the 31st of May of thesame year. Awesome isn't it? Don't ask me how it came to be. There are four children—two boys and two girls of which I am the very first child and daughter (double honours you might say). There are so many times that she sacrificed her money and time just to make sure that we were doing well. There times she would even not buy the latest clothes in town in order to make sure we looked good and fed well.

Bamidele I. Kehinde

She started her teaching career on the 1st of February, 1980 in a state government primary school. She was later transferred to different secondary schools in the same state since she was employed by the government of that state. Her chosen career really rubbed off on us in the family. She gave us moral lessons, punished us when we offended, rewarded us when we did well and even had pet names for all her children. In retrospect, I look at our family as another class she had to be in charge of apart from her real students. I can remember my friends making jest of my cleanliness and meticulous character in secondary school and university by calling me 'teacher's child'. It is believed in our society that a teacher's child is always the disciplined one as his/her parent who is a teacher must have brought him/her up in a 'no-nonsense' manner or background.

She was a Christian who devoted her life to serving the Lord God. She attended the Saint Paul's Anglican Church and even became the first female president of one of the societies in that church. 'Mama Kay' as she was fondly called was a very kind, generous and loving woman. She loved her husband and children so much that she gave all she had to ensure that we are who we are today. She was such a loyal wife to her husband (my dad); a very wise and supportive mother for us (the children) and a strong pillar for the family as a whole. She exhibited so much wisdom, had many friends who she positively influenced, her home was opened to everyone and she lived her life by gaining satisfaction from helping others.

If all these were not true, I would not have written them neither would I have any book to author because there would not have been any lessons. At this point, I must say she was not a saint. Though she had her lapses (which everyone does have), she was still someone who was very amiable. Heaven's gain and our loss but all thesame, I feel very proud to have been privileged to come to this world through her. 'One in a million' is an understatement in describing who and what my mother was to us. These days, I tell my friends who have their mums around to take care of them very well. They can only live but once.

In the subsequent chapters, the lessons I learnt will be fully discussed and I hope that this book will go a long way in inspiring as many people as possible.

3

Lesson Number 1: Always put your family first

While we were growing up, I saw my mother taking extra care of her husband always. This puzzled me for quite a long time until I was of age and decided to ask her why she did this. She told me that a woman should always do this because a man/husband who takes very good care of his wife and children should in turn be treated like a king. Moreso, the arrival of children into the marriage should not make a woman 'forget' how to take care of her husband as it is obvious that she knew the man first before the children started arriving.

By saying 'family' in this lesson, I mean the nuclear family especially. It is true that we value the extended family system in African societies a lot but these days, with the infiltration of Western culture/civilization, this belief system has waned. This is not to infer that my mum neglected the extended family members. Infact, as the first child of her parents, she was always on the lookout for her siblings. However, we (daddy and the children) were most important to her. This is because she believed that children are gifts from God and must be well taken care of.

Bamidele I. Kehinde

I learnt from her that once the home is peaceful and everyone is at peace with one another, then I can go out there and be all I want to be. This is true as we see today that many children who turn out to be miscreants in the society are many times often than not from dysfunctional homes. The psychological effect of the existence of peace or lack of it in a home goes a long way in boosting or reducing the morale and self esteem of any child.

In putting her family first, mama made sure that she carried us along in everything she did. It was her own way of concretizing the love in the family. For instance on many occasions, she would ask for opinion on what type of home wares to buy, what model of car we loved most, the clothes we felt fitted her the most, what to do about a co-teacher who talks too much during working hours and so on. She gave us this privilege unlike many women today who would rather go and ask their friends outside first.

Mama made us realize that we (the children) are each other's keeper. She emphasized that none of us must take steps that the other siblings will not be aware of. A good example was what usually happened during school holidays. Mum had an habit of eagerly waiting for us to come home with our gist. We would all gather in the girls' room to tell her one by one what each one enjoyed or endured in the course of the school term. She would even tell us to teach her some slang that we used just so that she would not be lost in the conversation. Amazingly, she always listened to each person's gist and of course, this endeared her to us the more.

Bamidele I. Kehinde

There were so many times that mum gave up attending social functions just to spend time with us. Imagine she even came to our hostels to where we lived in school. When we were much younger, mum would put us all in her car and take us to visit as many friends of hers that we could visit. Infact, at a time, we knew the names and home addresses of many colleagues of hers. This was made possible because she put her family first. Many of her friends knew that she never joked with the wellbeing of her husband and children. She was not the type of mum who would neglect her family only to go partying with friends who did not so much adore their families. Today, we are better for it and hope to continue this legacy.

4

Lesson Number 2: Be contented with whatever you have

Mum always emphasized that we should be contented with whatever we have. She stressed this by telling us that it was not that we should be complacent instead of aiming higher but, we should not be covetous or jealous of another. Rather, at whatever stage we are in our lives, we must appreciate God for whatever He has given us and also aim higher instead of complaining about what we do not have yet or comparing ourselves to other people.

This she not only taught us but also put into practice. My mum lived the life of a contented woman. I never really saw her pressurizing my dad to get things she knew were not within his capacity. Many a times, mum taught us how to 'manage' and make good use of the resources within our reach instead of being depressed about those things others around us have or how wealthier than us they were. She instilled in us the need to make good use of what we have and at the same time, aspire (without cutting corners) for greater heights in each person's career path.

She never came home to complain about our lack of luxurious things or how many of her friends and their husbands have many cars/houses. Instead, she will make sure that we do not lack the necessities of life. Right now, I can recollect how my mum on many occasions came to visit me in the boarding house when I was in secondary school without bringing beverages or pocket money. There was even an instance when she came to visit me and all she brought was her bowl of rice and beans (this was actually meant to be the food she was to eat during the school break in the school where she worked). This was really a humbling experience for me because she was not afraid to make me know the situation of things at home. There are not so many mothers who will be this 'open' to their children.

Whenever I wanted to complain about one lack or the other, mum always reminded me to be grateful first, never get depressed because of the lack and know that things will not continue to be this way. That is, things are bound to get better. Oh, what a rare gem she was!

A common piece of advice that was never far from her mouth was "things will not always be like this, they will get better". She never encouraged us to be jealous of other people and their possessions, neither did she allow any room for comparism between us and the children of others in the neighbourhood. There were times that we went to school with just what we needed, no extras. By extras, I mean we could only afford the basic necessities without any extras but still fared well. This is not to say that my mum was a frugal woman. No, she only taught us how to adapt to situations of life as they came across to us. When there was plenty, she lavished on us and when there was little, she 'managed' the resources very well so that everyone had a share of these.

I must say at this point that this lesson has really helped me in life. Instead of being covetous or envious of another person, I would rather focus my attention on a better thing. I am not perfect but this vital lesson has helped me to channel my desires and the resources at my disposal to more fulfilling things.

Mothers, do not hesitate to teach your children this lesson and also put it into practice. It goes a long way in making one focus on the right things in life. There are so many mums out there who do not see anything wrong in a child who has the habit of covetousness. This is not meant to be so. It is not too late to correct a child from going the wrong way in life. There were times I even wanted things that belonged to my siblings but mama never allowed this bad habit to thrive in me. Now, I can look back and say by doing this, she made me a better person. These days, I am eager to give my siblings than being covetous of their belongings.

5

Lesson Number 3: Never hesitate to see Life as a Surmountable Mountain

Life as we all know always has hurdles which we need to cross if not, we will stay stagnant in one place. Infact, some people say that life is not fair. This chapter is not to list all what life is or is not but to give the reader an insight into how my mother helped me to see life as a mountain that can be surmounted.

My mum was someone who had a 'never say die' spirit. That is, there were so many times that I would have given up on various feats in life but she encouraged me never to give up nor turn my back on hurdles that I can cross if only I could put in extra efforts. Although my dad and my mum were supportive, my mum never failed to be an unwavering pillar of support for my siblings and I. We could tell her anything and we knew well that instead of discouraging us she would rather make us see reasons why we have to forge ahead.

I can remember when it was time to write my final exams in the secondary school, she was just all over me with pieces of advice that I could make it if I worked hard. There were days when I actually studied extra hard just to please her. She was a woman who was very quick to give praise to whoever deserved it. This motivated me a lot. My mum even danced around in the house when I passed these exams.

Mama taught me to see beyond the hurdles I face at any particular time. She would tell me, "You can scale through". And indeed, I have scaled through the various hurdles I have faced in life. When it was time to go for my Masters degree, the home front was not very rosy so I had to go with an amount of money that was not enough. I was not too happy as I had really envisaged that this second degree was going to be more luxurious for me than what my first degree was. On realizing how I felt, mum stood by me. She told me that life could be rough at first but if I do not back off from the challenges but face them, I will go a long way. Just like the old cliché, tough times never last but tough people do. Altogether, from this lesson she taught me, I got to realize that life is not a bed of roses neither totally full of thorns but I should not always expect that good things come easy. There are sometimes that I have to cross various hurdles before I am able to get them. I will never forget this lesson—it has always been a guiding light for me. If not, I wouldn't author this book. She made me believe in myself and in my capabilities. The very first time that she set her eyes on my article in one of the Nigerian newspapers, she was quite excited. She told me I can go far with my writing skills if I do not give up. And no wonder, here I am today.

At the time I collected forms for Masters degree, I was confused about the course to choose for various reasons. First, I was meant to choose a research course but due to the way it is prolonged in our Nigerian universities, I had to choose a taught Masters degree. Secondly, I wanted to go back to the department I graduated from but was told their lecturers are not willing to offer admission for taught programmes. This really put me in a tight corner. I therefore had to consult with my parents. In the process of discussing with them, my mum made a statement that really touched me. She said she had gone through my yearbook (the ones we made in my graduating class), and noticed that I wrote, 'To be a diplomat of great repute in the heart of international affairs' in the column for future ambition. She reminded me of this line and said that in whatever field/course I wanted to choose, I must never deviate from this dream of mine. Whatever path I choose to go in life must always point towards the direction of achieving this goal. Eventually, I ended up going for Public Administration which I have no regrets whatsoever for doing so.

I was listening to a man who once said that he allows his children to watch good cartoons because their minds are 'stretched' since in cartoons, there are a lot of possibilities. This act he said, will make the children to know that in life, if you can imagine it then, you can achieve it. I did not grow up to view cartoons this way but I sure do know that what this man taught his children by using cartoons was likewise done by my mum but in her own case, she used words of encouragement; moral support and words of wisdom.

I have come to notice through an unconscious research that children are closer to their mothers than to their fathers. This goes to show how a mother should realize the vital and positive roles she has to play in the lives of her children. Mark these words, "a mother who always encourages, motivates and speaks positive words into the lives of her children is in no small measure helping the children to improve their self esteem". This is not advocating for pampering from the mother's end rather, a mother should improve her children's lives with the right words. I make bold to say that mothers should try this out and see the positive results they will get. Attack the problems a child is giving you rather than attacking the child with negative words. For mothers who perhaps have been doing this, I congratulate you. You must have seen the good results. Therefore, tell as many other people as you can that if the right words (I mean positive words) are spoken into a child's life, these do not only boost his/her morale but make the child to see life and its hurdles as a mountain that can be surmounted!

6

Lesson Number 4: Know something about everything

Mama did not teach us this lesson just because she wanted us to be jack of all trades and master of none. She wanted us to have vast knowledge and not be restricted to only our own field/career path.

This was most demonstrated in our home when mum made sure that whether boy or girl, you had to know how to do every home chore. I can imagine that some readers are disapproving of this as they read this line but I tell you, it really helped my siblings and I. She taught both the girls and the boys how to do dishes, prepare meals for the whole family, go to the market for shopping even up to cleaning car and putting water in the radiator.

She never believed that there were some chores reserved for a particular gender. Her strong opinion was that every one of us was capable of doing any house chore if we really put our minds to learning how to do it. At first, when we were growing up, this did not go down well with my siblings and I. We felt she was just bothering us with what was not necessary but now, I know better.

Mama even told the girls to cut the grass around the house if the boys were not available and sometimes told the boys to go shopping whenever their sisters were busy at home with more important chores. I can remember a particular day when my brother had to go to the meat market. He came back very furious because he had met one of his classmates (a female) who had seen him and made jest of him as it looked strange to her that a man would come to the market instead of his sisters. Despite this, trust my mama, she still sent the boys to the market as she firmly stood her ground against gender/chore bias.

Another aspect of this lesson was how my mum taught the boys to always take good care of their room since both of them share the same room. She would tell them, "If the girls' room could be clean and well arranged, why not yours". Initially, the boys really complained as they felt she was breathing down their necks but she never backed off. There were days she even stood at the entrance of the room just to monitor how the boys cleaned their room. She was never an advocate of laziness or excuses. Oh I remember now. She rubbed off too on her husband—my dad. She taught him some feminine chores that he could help with while every other person was busy. At this juncture though, I thank my dad for being willing to be teachable. This really helped in our home. This lesson has helped me a lot because I have now taken it from the home front to every other area of my life.

Many mothers I must say have created invisible barriers among their children by being gender/ chore bias. Let the reverse be the case and you will see how amazing the difference can be especially if your children are still young and not adults yet. It is never too late!

The third aspect of this lesson is that she made us know that we can be independent individuals. This is not to say that we should neglect family members and friends but as individuals, when we are able to know something about everything, we would not have to wait for others to help us before we help ourselves. She outrightly instilled this lesson in us. Life she made us know, might not always offer helpers for/to us. She was not being pessimistic, she was only stating the obvious—the reality of life. For us girls, mama helped us to know that we cannot afford to be liabilities in the society least of all, in our husbands' houses when we finally get married. A girl child she believed must 'sit up' just like her male counterparts. Infact, she has more work to do because she needs to be gainfully employed so that she can assist her husband with the bills. She taught me how not to be a 'let's wait for daddy' kind of mum. So I had to learn as many things as possible. "Be independent and you'll gain respect from men", she once told me. "You do not have to totally rely on his resources when you can work to get your own", she continued. Indeed, these are true words. As it is now, in the Nigerian society and even in countries of the world, women can no more afford to totally depend on their spouses. They now also contribute largely to the running of the home especially financially.

7

Lesson Number 5: Sex Education—A Lesson to be learnt early in life

These days, it has been discovered that children do not get to be taught about sex and its attendant factors by their parents. Rather, they are filled in with various pieces of advice from people outside their home. This should not be so. Parents must fully take up this responsibility.

I thank God that early in life; my mum gave us sex education. She never saw it as a taboo subject like many parents do. Mama told the girls about how conception can take place unknowingly if the girl is not careful about her sexual activities with the opposite sex. While she told the boys of how they need to be watchful because at a certain age, they begin to produce sperms which will get a girl impregnated when the time is not right for such.

I can remember vividly when I had my first menstruation. Mama was so happy that she even put down the date in her diary. She said this is a very significant mark for the beginning of a fruitful womanhood. However, she did not hesitate to tell me about how I needed to avoid men as I could get impregnated. Infact then, there was this myth that if you were menstruating and a boy touched you, you will become pregnant instantly. This myth is gradually fading away. Mama taught me how to be very hygienic especially during times like these. She lectured me on the proper use and disposal of sanitary pads. She even went further to narrate the circumstances surrounding the birth of each one of us. This I must say, gave me an insight into what motherhood has to offer before I later got a better grasp of it during my biology classes in secondary school. Imagine this: she said she did not even have an idea of what exact part of the woman's body a baby came out from until it was time for her to give birth to her first child, me!

She never forgot to make mention of the fact that a girl or woman's body is quite delicate and as such, should be treated with utmost care. She bought lingerie for us, taught us how to care for our bodies and even told the boys (when they became teenagers) to stop wearing pants. Instead, she told them boxer shorts are more preferable—so as to avoid too much heat on their genitals. Their immediate reaction was embarrassment but they later got used to hearing such talks from her. Many parents need to take up the responsibility of giving sex education to their children—male and female. The world has gone past the time when this topic was seen as a taboo topic for discussion. A lot of teenage pregnancies will be reduced or even eradicated if parents do their work well.

8

Lesson Number 6: Respect People—Whoever they are

In African societies, especially in the Southwestern part of Nigeria, according respect to people is taken seriously. I am not saying that people in the other geographical regions here in Nigeria do not have respect but the Southwestern indigenes show it more. The girls go on their knees to greet elders while the boys prostrate flat on the ground to greet the elderly ones or generally those older than them.

However, this tradition has been watered down. It no longer holds sway like what it used to be. But for the sake of better understanding, respect (in the context of this book) means honouring people, whoever they are. As human beings, there is the tendency for us to relate with people who are of timber and caliber more than we would relate with people in the lower class. Moreover, who does not want to be known or seen with the crème de la crème of the society? Despite all this, my mum disabused my mind from taking on this tendency. She made me realize that anyone could be someone in life. That is, no one should be looked down upon.

Relate with people of high or low esteem with honour and respect. Greet people with all the cheerful attitude you can muster. She actually lived this way all her life. Mum even greeted the gatemen at the gate of the estate we live in as though they were very important. She saw everyone as an important personality. This stunned me and made me to wonder why she had so much regard for everyone who came her way or those she came across. I am not saying that the gatemen were not important at least, if not for them, who would be manning the gates. But the fact that my mum could relate well with people from different walks of life was a lesson of life I had to learn from her.

Having noticed this behaviour of hers, I decided to question her and her reply was "nobody should be looked down on because anyone can become someone tomorrow. If you have been good to them, they will also be good to you". She also made mention of the fact that as a woman who would get married someday, I should cultivate this good habit as it will help me to relate well with all my in-laws whether they are good to me or not. She believed that it is not only those in-laws who are good or who I like that should be treated well and respected but every one of them should be respected. This attitude will help a lady to find favour in the sight of her in-laws.

In addition, she took the act of greeting very seriously. She believed that greeting people properly was another form of showing respect. In those days when we were growing up, before doing any house chore, my siblings and I would go to our parents' room in the morning to greet them. Whenever any of our parents was coming back home from a trip or visit to another place, we would run outside to greet them and even carry their bags inside the house. This habit was also extended to whoever visited our house. It was my mother's belief that there was no one who does not deserve to be greeted and respected. Along with this lesson came the habit of knowing how to say 'thank you' for every kind gesture shown. Our parents taught us how to say 'thank you'. To them, no kind gesture was too small to be appreciated. Infact, there were times that we were scolded just because we failed to be appreciative. As time went on, we had no choice but to be used to saying 'thank you' and 'I am sorry' as the case may be.

My advice to parents is that they should help their children to know how to be appreciative and to show it as many times as they can. It has been discovered that some children do not even say 'thank you' to their parents how much more to outsiders. This should not be so. From the very early stage of life should parents start giving their children this vital lesson. Someone who shows appreciation always will no doubt receive more kind gestures or gifts. This is a basic fact of life!

9

Lesson Number 7: Be Open Handed or Generous

I can imagine right now that some readers are wondering why this should be a lesson. Who does not know that it is good to give? But I tell you, there are many people who know this but do not do it.

Being open handed or generous comes naturally to some people while for others, it is a lesson that must be learnt. My mum had always known that it is good to give (be generous) but it was when she got married that her husband helped her to hone this skill. She once told us that daddy taught her how to be generous and she then decided to teach us too. My mum was so generous that there were times I got angry at her for giving such things out when she could still keep such for my siblings and I. She would then respond, "give and you will see it coming back to you in multiple folds". Mum gave from clothing right up to foodstuffs in her food store. Most times she gave and never expected such people to give something back in return. And also, whether you were richer or poorer than her, she would still give you. It was her belief that it was good to share with others whatever you have as there is this form of happiness or satisfaction within you that you have been able to bless others.

I can remember vividly how mum scolded us whenever we came back home with the remaining beverages we took to boarding house. She scolded us because she felt we could have given such things to those who did not have instead of coming back home with them. "Couldn't you look for someone who needed this?" she would ask. As a result, we could not help but cultivate the habit of giving.

Apart from giving to people whether they were richer than her or not, she also made it a point of duty to give the choicest things and not remnants. She was of the opinion that if you want to give, do it wholeheartedly and do not give what was spoilt (and better thrown away) or what more or less looked like a rag. Really, I can say that we are still reaping the benefits of this act of hers even after her departure. More so, we are continuing this lofty legacy of hers as it is evident that indeed, it pays to give than to receive. This is a natural law of nature that no one has been able to refute.

If you are holding this book right now and the lesson discussed in this chapter is something you have not been doing then, I guess this is a good medium to use to convince you that you should start giving. At times, what you need to give can be immaterial. For instance, learn how to smile at people, give people good advice, give someone a hug or a pat as the case may be and I bet you will realize that helping others or giving to them can bring so much satisfaction to you. At least, there are people who gain their happiness in life by helping or giving to people. Start today, it is never too late. Well, for those who know this natural law and have been putting it to use, they can confirm the fact that it is a tested and trusted law of nature. Usually, it is not what you give that comes back to you or the person you give who pays you back but definitely, you will be blessed in return.

I thank God for using my mum to teach me all these lessons. Now you know why I wrote at the beginning that her words of advice and these lessons are worth more than all the gold in the world to me. She has a place in my heart that no one can ever take away from me. I am so blessed to have her as my mother. Oh, what a privilege! Right now, I am not married but I believe that one day, my children and grandchildren will read this book and join me in celebrating the woman through whom I came to this world.

Finally, I feel so privileged and very grateful to God that I can use my writing skills to bless the world through this book. It is as much a blessing and source of inspiration to me as it would be to as many people who will take the time to read the book. Remember, reading the right literature and good books enriches us. And please take care of your parents because they might not be around for too long.

Tributes from Dad, my Siblings and I

Olusola, shortly after our wedding 29 years ago, you endeared yourself to my heart as a result of your humility, cooperation and the practical expression of your readiness to make our family a happy and united one. Your solid support for me through thick and thin and your support for the children during their formative years (especially) till your last day will linger on in my memory. You assisted in making our home and my job stable because there was always peace in our home. It is definite that if the home fails, the job will also crumble. I pray that God will continue to sustain the peace you left behind in the family.

It is pleasing to hear good remarks being made about you by the colleagues you have worked with, members of your society in church etc. It is very painful to lose you at the time you are needed most in the family. However God knows best.

Sola continue to rest in perfect peace till we meet to part no more!

Your Husband, Kolawole.

Olusola Oladele Kehinde a.k.a. Mama Kay. I really thank God for the life you lived, you were a strong pillar for your nuclear family; a favourite among your friends, a gem of inestimable value to your siblings/mother and an uncompromising ally for your husband.

On the day you had your last breath; I wish I was right by your bed side to stop death from taking you away if only it was possible. You were strong and fought the sickness with so much faith that we got encouragement and wisdom from you even while on the sickbed. Mama Kay, if I have the chance to come back to life the second time, I will still want you to be my mother. You taught me never to give up; you encouraged me with words of wisdom that were so timely in different phases of my life. You taught me how to be a mother even when I did not need such lessons yet. You were not a covetous woman; you made me see life as a mountain I should always surmount; I got my beauty from you, oh beautiful woman of Ekiti!

So much encomium have been poured in by different people about how you were an embodiment of good character. I thank God for all these but most of all, I know you are resting in the bosom of our Lord Jesus Christ. This is my greatest and only consolation; that we will meet again at the feet of our Lord Jesus Christ.

If all I have to do is run, then I will run the Christian race very well, Mama Kay. I want to see you again and if this means being more committed, I will. Heaven is the ultimate/final place for us all. I do not believe you are dead, you are only asleep. Sleep on my dearest mother till we meet again.

Daddy, my siblings and I greatly miss you. Thank you for being the best wife and mother this earth has ever had!

Your Daughter, Bamidele.

What else can I say, but 'thank God'.
I am grateful for the life you lived
For those lives you touched
For the love and care you always showed me
For your generous spirit and big heart
You were always there for me
You loved me, believed in me
You taught me contentment, resilience, tolerance,
humility, love and respect for others
Everyone you met, young or old, you always valued
You were ever ready to lend a helping hand to those
in need
Your strong and resilient spirit even in distress
Was a source of encouragement to me
Your smile, your contagious laughter
Will always remain a sweet memory
I'll always feel proud to be your daughter
Though I thought we would have many more years
together
I am glad you are resting now, in a better place
And I remain eternally grateful to God
For blessing me with such a mother as you

Your Daughter, Damilola.

Dear Mother,

It is true that good people don't always live long because they are too precious to God, so are you too, and that was why you were translated to Him in the early hours of Sunday, 6th March, 2011.

I had woken up that Sunday morning praying fervently for you like I always did, not knowing that you were already doing the same for me from the great beyond. Indeed it was a day that would go into the annals of history. I earnestly prayed for the miraculous only to be greeted with the inevitable.

Mummy, beautiful was indeed your name, wonderful you really were to me. I see you every day in my dream since you left me and my family. I remember with a nostalgic feeling our conversation on the 4th of January, 2011 when you admonished me about life issues, determination, resilience, hard work and faithfulness to God, I couldn't help but shed tears because I would not see you again for such friendly chats.

To say that you were an embodiment of humility, diligence and commitment is to say the least but most importantly, "the obvious". I remember how very often I quarrelled with you because I disagreed with the way you went out of your way to greet and visit people.

You saved me from tyranny, you taught me hard work, you made me fear God and people, you instilled in me the culture of respect, obedience and diligence at all times. You many a times inconvenienced yourself to give us life's comfort. You could do anything within your power to satisfy the needs of your children. In times of need, a mere look at you could give one hope for the future. You were intolerant of pride, deceit and laziness. You were indeed a wife and mother in the real sense of the word. You fought gallantly like the heroine that you were in the latter days of your life, you gave life a shot with an unprecedented zest, determination and poise. You were indeed a great pillar to Daddy and us.

Now, the sky looks very blue anytime I see it, and then I know you are smiling down upon me—one of the very important reasons to carry on with determination in life. As I continue to surmount the challenges of life without you, I am more determined to attain that enviable height you would have wished for me in your life time. I promise to immortalize you by living for what you've always preached. I will always keep the name of the family in dignity and utmost respect.

Mama Kay, if it is true that the departed ones with children don't sleep, then I expect you to always lead and guide in every decision I make.

I take solace in the fact that you're presently with Christ and you are praying for us mere mortals who do not know what tomorrow holds. Therefore, I shall not grieve.

I LOVE YOU MUM.

Your dear Son, Ayodeji.

Mum, I was told when I got back from school that you called my name and asked after me severally. What a rude shock it was when I was told about your transition. Dear Mother, I really miss you. You shielded me like an eagle would do for her eaglets; you cared for my every need as humanly possible as you could. All my friends tell me all the time that I am blessed to have such a mother like you.

You could read my expressions so well even when I failed to voice out. You knew what type of clothes and colours fitted me the most, you had listening ears even for the most trivial gist I had to tell. Oh mum, I know for sure that no one can replace you in my life. I never expected that your sickness will be unto death but God knows why He decided to take you away now. Indeed, you are a rare gem and an irreplaceable backbone for me. I can see you smiling down at me right now.

God in His infinite mercies will keep us and we shall meet again at the feet of our Lord Jesus Christ. Amen

Your Son, Ifedayo.

About the Author

Bamidele Kehinde is a young lady who was born in Ibadan—the largest city in West Africa and a major city in Oyo State, Nigeria. Born on the 31st of May, she hails from Ekiti State as a full blooded Nigerian.

She was born into the family of Mr. Julius Kolawole Kehinde and Mrs. Olusola Oladele Kehinde. She attended both primary and secondary schools in Oyo State but later moved to Osun State for her university education, all in the Southwestern part of Nigeria. She studied History and International Relations (double honours) and bagged a Bachelor of Arts (B.Arts) degree in the second class upper division. In the year 2010, she further proceeded to the same institution for her Masters degree in Public Administration (MPA). This prestigious institution is the Obafemi Awolowo University, Ile Ife.

As the first child and daughter in the family, she has three wonderful siblings who are all doing well in their respective fields in life. Protecting the family name is a legacy that each member of the family holds very dear. Bamidele is a Christian lady who believes in the Word of God and in God. She believes in the sovereignty of this awesome God.

Presently, she lives and works in Lagos—the commercial nerve centre of Nigeria. She works in a consultancy firm but hopes to divert later on into other industries of the various sectors of the economy. She loves to: do still-life drawing, listen to the radio, write articles, throw open meaningful conversations, surf the internet and achieve set goals. She also wants to travel to as many choice places as possible all over the world.

Even though she is not married now, she hopes that one day when she does, she will get to show her children this book about her mother since they couldn't get to meet her before her death!